PRESENTED TO:

C. Greiser

FROM:

S. Zamudio

DATE:

2/1/2020

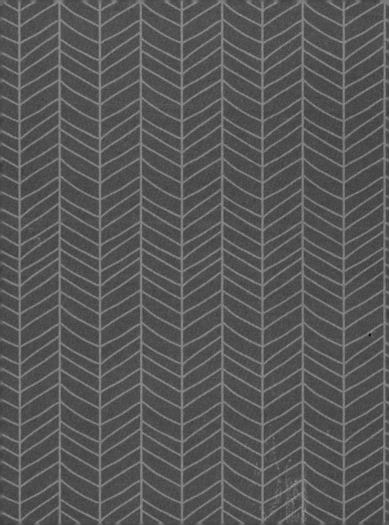

YOU KNOW YOU'RE A

DAD

A BOOK FOR DADS WHO NEVER
THOUGHT THEY'D SAY,
BINKIES, BLANKIES, OR CURFEW

HARRY H. HARRISON JR.

THOMAS NELSON
Since 1798

© 2017 Harry H. Harrison Jr.

Published in Nashville, Tennessee, by Thomas Nelson. Thomas Nelson is a registered trademark of HarperCollins Christian Publishing, Inc.

Thomas Nelson titles may be purchased in bulk for educational, business, fund-raising, or sales promotional use. For information, please e-mail SpecialMarkets@ThomasNelson.com.

ISBN: 978-0-7180-8707-4

Printed in China

17 18 19 20 21 TIMS 6 5 4 3 2 1

This book is dedicated to Dr. Peter Przekop.
His amazing work made everything possible.

CONTENTS

INTRODUCTION

A guy walks into the labor room a man, and then, in one of the most traumatic, intense, life-altering events imaginable, he turns into a father. Instantly. And if this is his first child, his only preparation has been watching his wife read books about babies. So, in other words, he knows just a little more about being a dad than he does about being a potted plant. But in reality, nothing can prepare him for being a father except being a father. The fact is, every day prepares a dad for the next day because every day contains signs that he is a dad. This is a book about recognizing those signs.

1

YOU KNOW YOU'RE A
DAD WHEN YOU THINK
DIFFERENTLY THAN
MEN WITHOUT KIDS

You know you're a dad when . . .

You secretly panic after hearing the news that she's pregnant, then are overcome by feelings of nausea, doom, and the need to hold on to the remote control. This condition can last minutes or through college graduation.

•

You feel overcome at the third month when you learn your baby—who in your mind is a just a cute little blob in your wife's belly—is four inches long and weighs one ounce; has arms, hands, fingers, feet, and toes; and can open and close her fists and mouth and suck her thumb. The circulatory and urinary systems are even working. She's *alive*!

•

You start giving back rubs to your pregnant wife every single night. Foot rubs are not out of the question either.

•

You realize your wife wants you to show unrestrained joy at the little line on the stick, while you deal with the reality that that line means your future savings just took a $400,000 hit.

•

She wants to have a deep, meaningful discussion about whether *Brook* is a boy's name or a girl's name—with about two minutes to go in a tight game.

•

You buy your unborn baby a baseball glove
while everyone else is buying teething
toys and baby mobiles and Binkies,
because no matter the sex of your baby,
he or she is going to be a shortstop.

●

You wake up in a cold sweat over the
thought of your increased responsibility.
This is called "delayed onset maturity."

●

You watch your man cave turn pink because
you've been told it's now the nursery.

●

Despite the fact that your wife's doctor
has delivered thousands of babies, you
wonder if that's quite enough experience.

•

You never miss one of your
wife's appointments with the ob-
gyn, even if it means pushing an
important client meeting back.

•

You tour the maternity ward with
your wife and realize your honeymoon
hotel wasn't this luxurious.

•

You spend the time learning what the
health insurance will pay. Some births cost
a big-screen TV. Some cost a small car.

•

You are stunned by the cost of baby
furniture because you think small
furniture means small prices, so really,
how expensive could that small stuff be?

•

Suddenly it seems like those
commercials for life insurance
are talking directly to you.

•

You decide only the best crib will
do for your baby—and then, after
pricing out cribs, you wonder just
how important a crib really is.

•

You believe you can put a crib together in an hour, tops, then open the box to find two thousand parts and eight pages of instructions, and then, after six hours, realize you're missing the three most critical pieces.

•

You finally get the crib together at 6:00 a.m. only to learn you need to spend more money. On a mattress. Actually, on two of them. Not to mention the sheets and a bumper pad, whatever that is.

•

Even though your baby is the size of a golf ball at the moment, you grasp that this fatherhood thing requires a man, so you sell your old Pokémon card collection to start a college fund.

•

You know the only way you can be the kind of father God wants you to be is to ask for His help.

•

You celebrate the fact that she's beginning to show.

•

You give her the side of the bed near the bathroom because she's scurrying there most of the night.

•

You stagger out of bed at 2:30 a.m. because she has a craving for cottage cheese with French dressing and chili peppers. You try not to gag while your wife gulps it down in bed. You also keep a can of room spray for this very purpose.

●

You both realize that last month's
maternity clothes don't necessarily
fit this month's maternity body.
So it's off to the mall again.

●

You're overcome with the urge to talk
to other men about baby names.

●

After you've looked at over a
thousand baby names, you name
her after your grandmother.

●

You learn that arguing with a
pregnant woman is suicidal.

●

Without saying a word, you quietly air out the house after she takes her prenatal vitamins.

●

You're not thrilled about killing a good Saturday afternoon attending a baby shower—but you know it's important to your wife, so you give her a big hug and tell her you're happy to attend.

●

You care enough to lie and tell her she looks better with thin hair.

●

You start watching other men with their kids and deciding which dads you want to imitate. And definitely which ones you don't.

•

You leave a hotel at 1 a.m. to grab the red-eye so you can be at the ultrasound the next morning.

•

You start paying down all the debt you've piled up till now. Which is challenging in light of the cost of a crib.

•

You read the sports commentary to your wife's stomach no matter whether your baby is a boy or a girl.

•

You constantly reassure a panic-stricken
mom at 3:00 a.m. that you do have
a plan for the family finances, and
urge her to go back to sleep. (It helps
greatly here to actually have a plan.)

•

You stop any TV commercial with a baby,
wait thirty seconds, then fast-forward
through it knowing that failure to follow
this exact plan will result in ten minutes
of tears from your pregnant wife.

•

You continually tell her she's going
to be a great mom. And after nine
months you tell her she is a great
mom for the rest of her life.

●

You come home from work early to say hello to your baby by tapping on your wife's stomach. And your biggest joy is when your baby pushes back.

●

You make the unfortunate discovery that all moms have a deep genetic need to whack off all their hair. When this happens, you tell her she looks great.

●

You say, "Good morning" and "Good night" to your wife's stomach. Perfectly normal.

●

You wrestle with whether to calmly fill out the myriad of hospital and insurance forms piling up on your desk now instead of watching football, or wait until your wife's water breaks all over the admissions room floor and you have to furiously fill them out while she's giving birth. It's not an easy call.

•

You find yourself nauseated, gaining weight, and feeling a bit moody. You have sympathetic pregnancy. Resist the urge to cut off all your hair.

•

For the first time in your life, you stand in the grocery store aisle, suspiciously reading the nutritional label on jars of baby food. And you're not sure you like what you see.

•

You wake up in the middle of the night and find your wife—a fierce trial lawyer during the day—next to you, cross-stitching a quilt for the nursery. This is called "nesting." Don't interfere. Just go back to sleep.

•

You discover underwear twice the size of yours in the washing machine and don't make a single comment.

•

You start visiting child care providers and grilling them like you're in the KGB.

•

You spend the last couple of months
of pregnancy watching videos of
complete strangers giving birth. (*This*
would probably be an excellent time
to fill out those hospital forms.)

•

Even though you think it's insane
because your baby isn't even born, you
have to start calling private schools
about their admission requirements.

•

You secretly wonder if her body
will ever return to normal. It will.
Maybe not totally, but 99.9 percent.
Okay, 97 percent. Whatever.

•

You start making a future budget and listing diapers, baby food, clothes, high chair, crib, doctor's visits, formula, and so on, before you get to the vacation fund.

●

You tell her she's beautiful in the ninth month. She needs to hear it. All the time.

●

Every time you're away from the house and your cell phone rings, you wonder if *this* phone call means, "Come get me! And hurry!"

●

You take your pregnant wife out for dinner and/or a movie as often as she feels like it. Going out will soon be just a sweet but distant memory.

•

You appreciate her fragile condition when she says she doesn't think ten blankets, seven sheets, two cribs, one layette, seven mobiles, two changing tables, baby furniture, push toys, pull toys, and two chests of clothes will be enough. So you go baby-stuff shopping with her again.

•

You try not to totally freak out when your baby's due date comes and goes and there's no baby.

•

You start reading *Consumer Reports* and comparing different cars and SUVs because side-impact safety protection suddenly matters to you.

•

You realize you have to decide between a Bugaboo and a 42-inch TV. Your wife, of course, has already decided. And she's not impressed that you don't know what a Bugaboo is.

•

You make a detailed plan about what to do when she goes into labor that would rival that of the D-Day invasion

•

You keep the "hospital" car filled with gas so you don't have to stop when the baby starts knocking.

•

You panic at the first sign of labor, only to learn it's false. Then feel a bit worried at the second sign of labor, only to learn it, too, is false. Then you're on the golf course when your wife calls, and you wonder if you should answer the phone.

•

You accept the fact that your wife will probably go into labor late at night at least three times. And that this is just a preview of what your child will do to your sleep.

•

You're watching the game when she starts having contractions again, and you wonder if you should panic or if you can just wait until the end of the fourth quarter and then race to the hospital.

•

In an effort to keep her calm as you're racing to the hospital, you ask her if she'd like to listen to rock music or a sports station. Seems neither is a good idea.

•

You try to time her contractions while driving to the hospital with your wife screaming, "Drive faster!"

•

You come to the realization that your usefulness in the labor room barely rivals that of a lampshade.

•

You learn your baby is coming in an hour and decide in the labor room that maybe you ought to thumb through a few of those child care books. Maybe fill out some forms.

•

You fight to stay calm while you're in the delivery room. You calculate how far it is to the bathroom if you have to throw up.

•

You're forced to give up the fantasy that you will be able to fix your wife's labor pains. You realize only the delivery of the baby can do that.

•

You find yourself sitting in the labor room
in the dark and listening to Pavarotti.
It does nothing for your mood.

•

During a long labor, you very subtly
sneak a peek at your phone to see if you
have any important e-mails or messages.
And, okay, to check the sports updates.

•

You start feeling guilty because you
forgot the aroma oils that she says are
the only things that will help reduce
her pain. Even though you got her
to the hospital in record time.

•

You listen to a woman—who has vowed for nine months that she wants natural childbirth—scream for pain relief after ten minutes of hard labor. It's okay. Her doctors won't be surprised.

•

You hold your wife's hand for five hours because she asks you to. You don't relax your hand even when it turns white and loses all feeling.

•

You are asked to cut the umbilical cord. You may or may not faint.

•

Your wife tells you to not even *think* of pulling out your phone and taking a picture until she has her hair done. Yes, this happens.

●

She tells you not to worry about taking a photo; she has a photographer coming for a glamour shot. Yes, this happens too.

●

You go on and sneak a picture that causes her embarrassment every time she sees it.

●

This newborn baby is put into your hands, and you simultaneously become terrified and fall in love.

•

You understand that God has
big plans for you. He chose you
to be the father of His child.

•

You start making promises to yourself
about the kind of man you're going
to be. Superman comes to mind.

2

YOU KNOW YOU'RE A
DAD WHEN EVEN THOUGH
YOU'RE A MANLY MAN, YOU
SPEAK IN BABY TALK

You know you're a dad when . . .

You anxiously start counting fingers and toes after delivery. Somebody has to.

•

You are mystified as to what a Binkie is even though your wife says you have five of them.

•

Suddenly, whenever you're out with your baby, you start meeting other men with babies. Who knew they were out there?

•

You no longer spend evenings and weekends on the couch. (Unless there's a baby sleeping on your stomach.)

•

You know happiness isn't a goal, but a consequence. Good grades make people happy. Helping others makes people happy. Self-respect makes people happy. Being potty trained makes people happy.

•

You understand that how dumb you are depends on the age of your child:

0 to 6 years old: Dad knows everything.

7 to 8 years old: Dad knows almost everything.

9 to 12 years old: Dad knows many things.

13 to 16 years old: Dad knows one or two things.

17 to 20 years old: Dad knows nothing.

21 to 23 years old: Maybe Dad does know one or two things.
24 to 25 years old: Actually, Dad knows many things.
Over 25: Dad knows everything.

•

You no longer spend every afternoon on the golf course. Or every weekend biking a hundred miles. Or every day working at the office for eighteen hours. Instead your new favorite hobby is being at home playing peekaboo with your baby.

•

You joyfully post five hundred photos of the birth, the mother, the baby, and the happy family on every social media site known to humankind.

•

You fill her room with flowers.
Not just a vase. Her room.

•

You come to grips with the fact that
more than a baby has been born.
So has a mother and a father.

•

You take your newborn into the hospital
chapel and offer your baby to God.

•

You phone brothers, sisters, distant
aunts, your friends, your insurance
agent, the lady at the grocery checkout—
everyone—the day the baby arrives. If
anyone is left out, feelings will be hurt.

●

You find out how long the insurance
company will allow your wife to stay in
the hospital. And you insist she stay there
and rest until the last possible minute.

●

You panic because you haven't read a single
book, and in the excitement you've forgotten
everything you've learned in delivery class,
so you bribe a nurse to show you how to
change your baby's diaper. This lesson
will give you the illusion of knowledge.

●

You apply for your baby's Social
Security number when you fill out her
birth certificate because now you have
a bouncing baby tax deduction.

•

You learn to handle baby with
care. But definitely handle.

•

Overnight, you up your values a notch.
Maybe two or three notches.

•

You get mother and child home and
inside, and you realize you're officially
on your own. You marvel that they don't
even require a license for parenthood.

•

You take the week off after your baby
comes home because you have seven
days to learn how to be a father.

●

You realize you have to let your wife teach you child care. After all, she's read all the books. You've been reading *Sports Illustrated*.

●

You realize that all the stupid stuff your wife bought to simply change the baby— like wet wipes, diaper pins, a lined trash can with a lid, new outfits, and diaper rash cream—are, well, really important.

●

You put your child's wants, needs, and desires ahead of your own wants, needs, and desires. Every day.

●

You stare at your baby all night the first night home. And most of the second.

•

You spend their first year or so teaching them to stand on their own two feet. Then you spend the next twenty years or so reinforcing that lesson.

•

Wherever you are in the room you try to make eye contact with your baby, even though he can't focus beyond his nose yet.

•

You decide even though your baby is only a week old, she needs to exercise. So you gently move her arms and legs up and down and in little yoga poses.

●

The first night your baby is in his own room, you stay up all night listening to the baby monitor.

●

You refuse to say "sippy cup" in public.

●

You start a 529 college savings plan. You're excited that $300 a month will turn into more than $110,000 in seventeen years, but then you learn that won't be half of what you need.

●

You gently hint to grandparents that contributions to the college fund will always make nice birthday gifts.

•

Out of desperation you hold a
peeing baby over the sink.

•

You swear you'll never carry a diaper bag, so
you force all of its contents into a duffel bag
or briefcase. Too late you realize what your
briefcase will smell like for two to three years.

•

You crawl home from the office exhausted,
collapse into your easy chair, and then
wonder why your behind feels wet.

•

You hold your baby upside down above
your face—while your wife fusses at
you and your baby screams in delight—
and get drooled on for your trouble.

•

You wake up thinking the entire house smells of dirty diapers, so you make a substantial investment in room spray, carpet spray, even spray deodorant. Your wife, however, thinks you've lost your mind because she doesn't smell a thing.

•

You stage a baby formula taste test. Because you want to know.

•

You sample pureed beets baby food because you know you've put worse things in your mouth, and then decide, no, you actually haven't.

•

You drop your baby off at the grandparents' house and take your wife away for the weekend, which you both promptly sleep through.

•

The diaper strips don't do the job, so you go frantically hunting for the masking tape.

•

You're quietly pleased with yourself for teaching your baby two words: *Da Da*.

•

At 2 a.m. you put a crying baby on your shoulder, plug your iPod into your ears, crank it up, and rock your baby back to sleep.

•

You change her diaper, and while it doesn't really fit, you give good odds that the diaper won't fall off.

•

Your wife takes you to the baby store to buy a colorful baby mobile that you figure is eighty more dollars down the drain— until you realize it can buy you twenty extra minutes of sleep in the morning.

•

You learn baby code. For instance, "colic" is shorthand for "screaming, unhappy baby, 3:00 a.m. rocking, and worried sick and exhausted parents."

•

You realize small children create a magical time in a dad's life. And you pray you won't miss a minute of it.

•

You foolishly think every now and then that you've bought *everything* a baby could possibly need for the next two years and that the money hemorrhage will stop. You later discover that her teenage years make this look like a bargain.

•

You start losing hair to little hands pulling on chest hair, nose hair, head hair, beard hair, and—the most painful—leg hair.

•

You gently roughhouse with your
child even though your wife thinks
you will damage her forever.

•

You decide the baby can only ride in the
Mom Car so that your car will not be
abused with spit-up, spilled baby formula,
leaky diapers, smelly car seats, and half-
eaten animal crackers stuck to the floor.

•

You resolve to spend time with your
child—real, meaningful, "I could
be on the golf course" and "I got
home from the office early" time.

•

You're barely able to perform semiconscious 3:00 a.m. feedings even though you used to be able to party all night.

●

You come to the realization that babies cry when they're hungry. When they have gas. When they're tired. When they're lonely. And pretty much for no reason at all that you can discern.

●

Surveying your once-cool condo that's now besieged by your baby's bassinet, crib, diaper boxes, toys, stroller, car seat, and clothes—you decide you like the new look.

●

You decide baby talk is macho.
Really. Dadagoogoo.

•

You spend hours trying to settle
down your screaming daughter, with
no success, when you decide that a
crying or fussy baby could have made
even Dr. Spock feel incompetent.

•

You start sleepwalking at the office
because you're so tired from the nighttime
feedings, rockings, and burpings.

•

You jog around the lake with your
baby and feel confident you have the
hottest Euro stroller on the block.

•

You challenge another dad to a stroller race. With babies strapped in. You do not share this with your wife.

•

Despite everything you vowed, you now wear a baby carrier all over town. Yes, you look ridiculous.

•

You learn that it will take your wife the next nine months to recover from the last nine months.

•

You stow away your golf clubs for a while. Your nights and weekends are now booked.

•

You lift a crying baby out of his crib
and sing to him at night. You know
one of the great things about babies is,
they don't care if you sing the Beatles,
Twisted Sister, or Taylor Swift.

●

You find yourself marveling at how
something so tiny can wake the dead.

●

You have a staring contest
with a six-month-old.

●

While pushing your son in a jogging
stroller for six miles, you realize
that one day he'll outrun you.

●

Your most favorite time of day is
falling asleep while your baby sleeps
on your chest. This is magic.

•

You watch your daughter plop down while
trying to walk and you resolve not to miss
the smallest details of your baby's life.

•

You've convinced yourself that you
change just as many diapers as
your wife although studies indicate
you're not even in the ballpark.

•

You swore you'd never do it, but you find
yourself sprinting across the store during
Black Friday in the hunt for this year's hot toy.

•

You start researching the cost of good child care and learn that it costs as much as sending him to Yale.

•

You tour prospective child care facilities that have installed camera monitors you can watch online; then you go to the office and watch the video feed all day.

•

You volunteer to teach Sunday school because that's where the best babysitters come from.

•

You get your baby to burp and suddenly you feel like your life means something.

•

You realize a day with clients,
meetings, business lunches, and
conference calls sounds like a spa
vacation compared to being at home
alone all day with a fussy baby.

•

You learn thirty minutes before
an important client meeting
that strained beets don't wash
off of white business shirts.

•

You emerge from the baby's
bath time wetter than the baby.
And both of you had fun.

●

You remind Mom that the family can go out to eat in the evening because babies can sleep anywhere. Then you end up holding a wailing baby all the way through dinner.

●

You unload your briefcase at a meeting and find a Binky. You think those little suckers are everywhere.

●

You realize your relationship with your wife is changing. Profoundly. It's no longer just about the two of you.

●

You realize that when a baby comes, the in-laws do too. Usually to stay for a while.

•

You understand that grandparents are the best babysitting deal around.

•

You just smile and nod when your father-in-law says your baby looks a lot like his side of the family.

•

You finally accept the fact that your home looks like a day care center.

•

You develop the unique ability to change a baby on your lap while you sit in a stall in the men's room. An unrecognized accomplishment in fatherhood.

●

You suddenly and inexplicably start dropping the word *potty* into conversations.

●

You put a baseball in your baby's crib. And a football. And a soccer ball.

●

After days and nights of research, you think you'll save money by buying diapers online, but the plethora of brands, sizes, shapes, materials, and deals sends you to Walmart to buy whatever's on sale.

●

You learn to do things one-handed while also carting your little one, like carrying five bags of groceries in one hand and your child in the other.

•

You feel someone crawling up your leg—and using your leg hair as grips—as you watch football.

•

You learn to trust your instincts. This will work especially well during your child's adolescence.

•

You realize your primary job is to convince your kids they can stand up without you.

•

You've become your child's entertainment center.

•

You show your child the intricacies
of dunking an Oreo into a glass
of milk and then eating it.

•

You gather all the kids on your lap and
watch the *The Muppets* on YouTube.

•

You pray, pray, and pray and then realize
that, yes, God will help you be the father
He wants you to be. You just had to ask.

•

You get more respect from your boss
than you do from your two-year-old.

•

You wonder how you can run a successful company, manage one hundred employees, and make a profit every quarter, yet fail to get a two-year-old into the bathtub.

•

You collapse in bed exhausted, realizing that a two-year-old has more energy than you.

•

You read the stock news to your kids at breakfast from your iPhone. You dream of the day they'll check the Dow for themselves.

•

You don't hesitate to use the words *no, never, absolutely not,* and *because I'm your father.*

•

You're sitting in a closet with the lights off and a flashlight on, telling ghost stories to wide-eyed kids, and realize that this could be the most hilarious time of your life.

•

You stay home late in the morning to bake hot sweet rolls for your kids, and you make sure there's plenty of butter and cinnamon, and your four-year-old takes a bite and announces Mom's cooking is better.

•

Suddenly it dawns on you
that fatherhood is cool.

•

You're the first adult your wife
has talked to in ten hours.

●

You give piggyback rides on demand,
even if you're in a suit and tie, even if
you have the flu, but you draw the line
at carrying three riders at once.

●

You believe the greatest invention of
all time is a DVR. Ostensibly so you
can record children's shows. In reality
so you can watch your favorite TV
show when your kids are asleep.

●

You resolve to never try to reason with
anyone who isn't potty trained.

•

You calmly let your two-year-old start dismantling a department store display rack to see what happens first: the display gets demolished or a panicked salesclerk shows up to actually wait on you.

•

You are working late and get a tearful phone call from your five-year-old saying she can't go to bed without a hug from you. Time to load up and head home!

•

You admire the scars on your daughter's knee rather than being alarmed by them.

•

You spend hours teaching a three-year-old boy to aim first, then pee.

•

You're forced to explain to your daughter why she doesn't need to lift the toilet seat like her brother.

•

You have your child help clean up the spilled milk. Think of this as a life lesson.

•

You read something to your kids every night. Even if it's the sports section.

•

You watch your kids have more fun with a box than with the $200 toy that came in it.

•

You find that reading time often
develops into tickling time.

•

You resort to asking the teenage
cashier with face jewelry if she
babysits in her spare time.

•

You have to explain to a three-year-old
that while it's okay to run around naked in
the backyard, she needs to put something
on before dashing out the front door.

•

You bundle up whiny kids and take
them outside in the pouring rain to show
them that rainy days are great fun.

•

You show your kids how to stomp on
a spider. And tell them not to freak
out over the crunching sound.

•

You use simple math to figure out that
if you have more than two kids, you're
outnumbered. You have to shift from
a man-to-man defense to zone.

•

You give up HBO for about fifteen years
because you don't want to have to worry
about what your kids are watching.

•

You give your kids swimming lessons. Then you take them into the pool and have them swim to you, time and time again. Till they can swim like tadpoles.

●

You spend many afternoons teaching a four-year-old to face her fears. This is one of the most important jobs a father can tackle.

●

It's you who suggests cartoons because you think one more visit to Daniel Tiger's Neighborhood could make you go postal.

●

You test, test, and test again your young children to be sure they know their first and last names, their address, your name, your cell phone number, their mom's name, and her cell phone number. It's like an SAT prep course around your house for a while.

•

You teach your three-year-old son when and how to call 9-1-1. And then apologize profusely to the nice police officer who shows up when your son tries it out for fun.

•

Even though you swore to yourself you would never do so, you start reading the dad blogs on the Internet and wondering if you would have liked those guys in high school.

•

You take on faith that a new trike should contain six, maybe ten pieces, tops, and it will be easy to assemble on Christmas Eve. Then you spend all Christmas Eve night putting together the five hundred pieces of said new trike, while your wife keeps yelling from the bedroom that you should have paid the store to do it.

•

You give up the playoff game to take your kids to a stupefyingly boring kid's movie— and they fall asleep ten minutes into it.

•

You pick up your kids from day care and wonder if the adults there intentionally douse your kids in grape juice before sending them home.

•

You play catch with a ball covered in glitter.

•

You find yourself lying on the couch
with a handful of Advil after doing
somersaults with your children.

•

You have reasons to regret you didn't teach
a five-ear-old that superglue is forever.

•

You happily spend Saturday mornings
in the doughnut shop, reading the
paper while your kids inhale chocolate-
covered bear claws and Coke.

•

You encourage your kids to feel your muscles because your wife refuses to. They are awed; she's unimpressed.

•

You convince a hesitant four-year-old that it's fun getting launched off your shoulders into a swimming pool— and then hours later beg the same child to let you out of the pool because you are exhausted and need Advil.

•

You encourage your kids to get up when they fall. This is a lesson that will serve them well the rest of their lives.

•

You tell your kids a little blood won't hurt them. In fact, you show them how to wipe it off their elbows or knees. Their mother, of course, is disgusted.

●

You tell your kids to deal with scrapes and bruises by doing the following:
"Walk it off!"
"Blow on it."
"Run it under cold water."

●

You let your child dress herself for preschool even if she emerges wearing a Batman costume. As far as you're concerned, she's dressed.

●

You spend the afternoon lying in the grass with your child and finding shapes and faces in the clouds.

•

You make whatever they'll eat for breakfast every morning. Doughnuts. Sweet rolls. Biscuits and eggs. Besides, milk will balance everything out.

•

You look your five-year-old in the eye and tell her there's nothing scary about going to the dentist, even though you haven't been in ten years because, well, thinking about it gives you nightmares.

•

After watching *The Muppets* for
two years, you decide Muppet
humor is really sophisticated.

•

You decide it's never too early to set high
goals, like medical school, so you sing to
your three-year-old the multiplication
tables so she'll memorize them.

•

You develop the unique ability to
not hear a child's whining.

•

Like a good parent, you say you'll
eat your okra if they'll eat their
okra and then realize at the first
bite that okra makes you gag.

●

You start vacuuming the house but turn it into a game of chase.

●

In desperation during a rainy day, you build a fort out of a sheet. The kids declare you the coolest dad ever.

●

You give an exhausted four-year-old fisherman a ride back to the car on your shoulders while you also carry the fishing rods and gear.

●

You find yourself saying, "Go outside and play" then lying down on the couch and taking a nap.

•

You find a four-year-old with
his baseball glove on waiting for
you when you get home.

•

After a full day of work and playing
with young children for three hours, you
fall asleep before the evening news.

•

You tell your four-year-old that we all must
set goals in life and that your goal for her
is medical school. She just looks at you.

•

You realize a sick toddler is preparing
you for raising a teenager: both are
sullen, depressed, and needy.

•

Suddenly you become the answer man. And if you don't know the answer, you make it up.

•

You start reading books to your kids using funny voices that cause them to collapse in laughter.

•

You take your five-year-old daughter into the toy store on her birthday and tell her she can keep everything she can grab in five minutes. You wouldn't dare do this with a ten year-old.

•

You make sure cell phones, car keys, iPads, iPods, and wallets are not touched by hands covered with peanut butter and jelly. You bat 50 percent here.

•

You see your child eat a worm and ponder whether this is info you want to share with his mother.

•

Every time you go outside to work in the yard, you hand your kid a spade and tell him to go dig a hole.

•

You smell the Mom Car every week to see if the leftover food, wet clothes, muddy boots, pet hair, and spilled milk have begun to ferment.

•

You institute the "No Throwing Up in Dad's Car" policy. What makes this remarkable is that you don't allow children in your car. But just in case . . .

•

You insist on using Mom's car to rush a sick child to the doctor because of the "No Throwing Up in Dad's Car" rule.

•

You talk to your kids no matter their age. All the time. About everything. Because you always want them to talk to you in the future

•

You sniff your child, then sniff your dog, and decide they've both been rolling in the same thing.

•

You know for sure that after a long day at work, at least one person in the world will be delighted to see you when you walk in the door.

•

You say to quarreling siblings, "I don't care who started it. I'm stopping it!"

•

You've learned how to bond over cookies and milk.

•

You believe it's time to take the training wheels off. In fact, that pretty much defines *fatherhood*.

•

You have to put a bandage on a skinned knee while your wife reminds you that taking the training wheels off was your idea.

•

You man up and pretend to eat a pie made of Silly Putty.

•

You turn the telephone sales call from overseas over to your four-year-old. Salespeople have quit calling.

•

You turn off the lights, give your kids a flashlight, and tell them a ghost story that makes them run to Mama.

•

Your toddler walks past the hall bathroom, into your bedroom, around the bed so he won't wake up Mom, and throws up on you.

•

You insist your son wears a bike helmet while you refuse to.

•

You come home and start wrestling with your kids, get them all excited—and then tell them to calm down so you can rest.

●

You start spelling words to your
wife when the kids are around.
Then you realize the kids might be
more literate than you thought.

●

You come home exhausted from
work and chores and errands, only
to have a five-year-old point out the
sunset that you somehow missed.

●

You take your kids to the library
and tell them that a library is
a place for smart people.

●

You wonder if you're saying no too much.

●

You actually believe (at least temporarily) that if you buy this one more stupid thing, your child will quit bellyaching about wanting stuff.

●

You call your kids as you're on the way to the office if you had to leave before breakfast. It makes their morning.

●

You stand in a conga line at the mall for two hours so your child can have a picture taken with Santa even though your Christmas spirit disappeared an hour earlier.

•

You record your kindergartener's concert instead of actually watching it. Then somehow erase the recording before you get it home.

•

You read Dr. Seuss books to her every night instead of the business reports you really need to read.

•

You put your kids' songs on your iPod and let them listen to it. Of course, if your toddler toddles out of the room with your iPod, you may never see it again.

•

You spend Saturday afternoon teaching your kids how to hold and throw a rock so it will skip at least three times across a lake.

3

YOU KNOW YOU'RE A
DAD WHEN YOUR TEEN
DOESN'T BELIEVE YOU
CAN DRESS YOURSELF
CAN DRESS YOURSELF

You know you're a dad when . . .

You set high expectations for your kids. And they meet them.

•

You are prepared to act the heavy. You know it's your job to say: "No." "Change your dress." "We don't use that language." "I brought you into this world, and I can take you out of it." And most important, "Get a job."

•

You realize you have to be your child's father. Not your child's best buddy.

•

You realize the importance of developing in your kids the belief that they can do it themselves.

•

You feel it's important to teach your kids to stand up for their rights. Which works fine until they stand up to you!

•

You hold tight to four words: *It's just a stage.*

•

You command your kids' respect. And reassure them of your love. At the same time.

•

You realize that even though your daughter isn't currently speaking to you, this is the time when she needs her dad the most.

•

You remind everyone just who makes the rules. And do so regularly.

•

You inform your fourteen-year-old that the privilege of driving will not hinge on turning sixteen, but on behavior, grades, the savings he's acquired, and your benevolence.

•

You hand your teen a list of dating rules. Really, really firm dating rules.

•

You remind your kids they are not the center of the universe. In fact, you point out to them that, really, you are the center of the universe, and their happiness depends upon yours.

•

You don't care that your kids would rather be seen with their friends than with you. They're part of a family, and families do things together.

•

No matter what she's wearing, you think your daughter's clothes are too revealing.

•

You point out to your kids that the avenues of success rarely run through Hollywood, rapping, or sports.

●

You think your son hasn't been in a good mood since he turned thirteen.

●

You tell your daughter that if she has something really important to say, say it. Don't text it. She texts you that she understands.

●

You want to be close to your kids without being their best friend.

●

You post an ad for military school on the refrigerator to get your kids' attention and only say it's an education option.

•

You explain that in nature there's no such thing as reward or punishment. Only consequences. This is also a house rule.

•

You learn it's amazing what teenagers in the backseat talk about. So you're happy to drive them around.

•

You remind your kids that homework is done with their minds alert, the lights on, and the TV off.

•

You realize your wife and your
teenagers are experiencing
significant shifts in hormones at
about the same time. Lucky you.

•

Your kids go to their mother for money
because they know you're a lost cause.

•

You put on something comfortable to wear
to the mall with your kids, but they say they
won't be seen with you until you change.

•

Your teenagers complain about
their curfew. You don't see why 9
p.m. isn't acceptable to them.

•

You talk to teachers, salesclerks, mail carriers, and servers with respect in front of your kids because you know you're shaping the way your kids will treat people in the future.

•

You don't want your kids to judge others by the cars they drive even though you know a Porsche would complete you.

•

You look at their chemistry homework and realize there is nothing you can do to help them.

•

You use the intercom to wake up truculent kids in the morning. Somehow they don't appreciate "Reveille."

•

You hire a private coach to make sure your child makes the team. Or the band. Because you believe in the scholarship dream.

•

You've held off buying new clothes, but your kids look like they've stepped off the pages of *GQ* and *Vogue*.

•

You wound your teen's feelings unintentionally. Because it's very easy to do right now.

•

You take a thirteen-year-old to the mall
on the thin hope he'll say more than
three words to you—and he spends
all his time on his cell phone.

•

You warn your teens that the heavens
will fall if they come downstairs on
Mother's Day without a gift.

•

You review a teen's priorities.
Some kids think a nice tan
should be their top priority.

•

You find yourself begging your
teen to take driver's ed so you
can quit being his chauffeur.

•

After much prayer and mental
preparation, you teach your kids
to drive. In their mother's car.

•

You feel like throwing confetti because
your teen drives around the block one time
and doesn't hit anything or anybody.

•

You review your teens on red light,
green light, stop sign, school zone. They
think they know. They don't know.

•

Your retirement fund goes up in smoke to pay the automobile insurance premiums for your teenage drivers.

•

You teach your teenager to drive in five o'clock traffic—in the pouring rain—before she gets her license because you want to make sure she can handle any road condition.

•

You ride with your teens as they learn to drive because their mother refuses to.

•

Your teen pleads for a new Beemer while you research ten-year-old pre-owned tanks.

•

Once they have their licenses, you allow your teens to drive the car—but they can't listen to the radio, they can't talk on their cell phones, they can't have more than one friend in the car, and they can't leave their zip code area. "But have fun!"

•

You buy your new driver a premium membership to AAA. Because the last thing you want to do is get off the couch at 9 p.m. to change a tire.

•

You tell your teen you won't be buying him gasoline. That's what jobs are for.

•

You try to show your kids how to change a tire even though you haven't changed one since your dad showed you how. Then, after thirty frustrating and futile minutes, you tell them not to lose AAA's phone number.

•

You have to explain to a teenager over and over again that *your* money is not *her* money.

•

You survey a dented fender and tell your teen you're not mad, but he has to get a job to pay for the car repair.

•

You see on the floor a note from one of your kid's friends, think about respecting her privacy, then read it.

•

You have to listen to a teenager say, "You don't respect my privacy," and you agree that, no, you don't. And try to figure out when you stopped being cool.

•

You sense that your kids believe you're incredibly lucky to have made it this far in life without their advice.

•

You buy each of your kids a share of stock and teach them how to track it.

•

You freely use words like *GNP, profit, earnings,* and *yield* at the dinner table.

•

You set an example on how to handle money. Which is hilarious to you when you consider what you were like before you had kids.

•

You explain to an unhappy teen that whining won't help anyone get money, but work will.

•

You look up from the couch and say, "Everything goes on sale."

•

You show your teen how to return stuff to the store and get money back. This is one of life's most important lessons.

•

You get final wardrobe approval.

•

You conclude that reminding a teenager to be grateful seems like a full-time job.

•

You honestly think a high school prom couldn't be that expensive. Then you learn that the limo alone is $1,200.

•

You tell your teen she's done a good job—when she's done a good job.

•

You sign up the kids to do community service with you. They'll say how bored they are. But they'll get the message.

•

You teach that selflessness is a cure for selfishness.

•

You let your kids see you fight through disappointment and failure.

•

You teach your kids there's a season for everything.

•

You let your kids find dignity in struggle.

•

You assure them that overnight successes
usually take about twenty years.

•

You lay down the law about speeding,
then get a speeding ticket.

•

You take comedy defensive driving
with your teenager because both of you
got speeding tickets. And you think,
all in all, it was a pretty good time.

•

You remind your kids that everything about Hollywood and TV and movies is fake. Especially the messages. They roll their eyes.

•

You give your son a driving lesson and catch yourself yelling at another driver.

•

You encourage big dreams.

•

You buy your teen *Rich Dad Poor Dad*.

•

You stay awake until everybody comes home. This is self-induced insomnia doctors will never be able to cure.

•

You show your kids by your actions that
the biblical secret to financial security is
giving away 10 percent of your wealth.
Even if that 10 percent is only five dollars.

•

You know the secret to getting a teen
talking is to take long walks with him.

•

You understand that your kids will
treat you like you treat them.

•

You talk with your kids about their
future. Make them think about it. Tell
them it's okay if their plan changes.

•

You choke up staring at your teen's
bulletin board over the memories
you and your wife gave her.

•

You buy *The Official SAT Study Guide*
thinking this is the ticket to Harvard. Then
you learn the cost of a Harvard education.

•

You wonder if they are learning
anything at school.

•

You realize there's a definite line between
trusting your kids and being an idiot.

•

You feel like other adults are blaming you if your teenager is having problems. The other adults are secretly worrying about the same thing with their kids.

•

You pop on your thirteen-year-old's iPod to hear what he's listening to and think, *Is this the same child I raised?*

•

You go upstairs to find out why she can't ever seem to make it down to breakfast on time, no matter what time she gets up.

•

You deal with your children's problems as they happen, not just hope things will get better.

•

You insist that everyone in the family be treated with respect, even the dog.

•

You teach them from a very young age that the very worst thing they can lose is your trust.

•

You spend all summer with teenagers in the house because you've grounded them.

•

You enforce house rules. *Your* house rules.

•

You monitor your child's computer usage from your office.

•

You make your kids think you're
angrier than you really are.

•

You remind your daughter that a cell
phone, acrylic nails, the tanning salon,
makeup, the car, and credit cards
are privileges. That can be lost.

•

You tell your son how to talk to
a judge—unless he's just dying
to go to the Big House.

•

You sit down with your kid's favorite
video game and do a body count.
Perhaps it needs to disappear.

•

You look at your child's problems
and wonder if you're the problem.

•

You pray for guidance. Daily.

•

You realize threats mean nothing.
Consequences mean everything.

•

You realize your child's been
talking for twenty minutes and you
have no idea what she's said.

•

You teach your values and morals to
your kids when they're young because
you know if you wait until they're
teenagers, you've waited too long.

●

You teach kids to tell the
truth by your example.

●

You tell your teens they can't date
anybody over twenty-one . . .
until they're over twenty-one.

●

You pray your kids learn that their actions
have consequences before they get older
and the consequences are more severe.

●

You lay down the law when dealing
with teenagers who are skilled
at finding loopholes in it.

●

You refuse to allow your teen a radar detector. The idea is to stay alive during the teen years.

●

You don't say everything you'd like to say in the heat of the moment. Instead you go out for a short run. Or a five-mile run. Maybe a ten-mile run if you're really mad.

●

You're consistent. With your love. With your discipline. You don't give your kids reasons to become confused.

●

You stand by your child without approving of his actions.

●

You listen to your kid's dreams, desires,
hopes, worries, fears, problems, and
conflicts. Without negative comments.

•

You accept that a lot of kids who
have problems in the teenage
world do fine in the adult world.
They just had a rougher start.

•

You take pride when your child
does the right thing.

•

You give your child the chance
to earn back your trust.

•

You're a source of hope to a confused
child. Or teen. Or mom.

•

You're trying to teach your teens to live
below their means, while you're taking a
second mortgage to buy a swimming pool.

•

You teach that with patience and
negotiations almost everything
can be had for less.

•

You have the Money Talk. This is
the talk where you tell your kids
they have to start earning money,
and they try to talk you out of it.

•

You come to grips with the fact that
you'll never be able to give your
family everything they want. A lot of
things, maybe. But not everything.
And that's no reason to feel guilty.

●

You're the financial role model. If
they see you being responsible with
money, they will be too. If they see you
MasterCarding Jet Skis and big-screens,
they will wind up in credit counseling.

●

You teach delayed gratification—
that Beemers and condos come to
those who work, save, and wait.

●

You realize you're going to have
to pay somebody to mow the yard
despite the fact that you have healthy
teenagers living at home.

•

You are being told by kids who do
as little as possible for an allowance
that they are being underpaid.

•

You point out that with free room,
free food, free use of the big-screen,
free handling of the remote, plus
free spending money, they're living
in the top 1 percent of the world.

•

You know that Mom is slipping
them money under the table—
and you're okay with it.

•

You face the dilemma of saving for
retirement right about the time
college tuition bills start arriving.

•

You worry your kids have it too easy.
But are grateful to God that they do.

•

You teach your kids to pay
their bills on time.

•

You teach your high schooler to handle
credit cards as if they're radioactive.

●

You teach financial literacy using terms like *profit, loss,* and *buyout* at the dinner table.

●

You teach your kids that putting money regularly into a savings account is a surefire way of getting rich slowly.

●

You buy your teen a subscription to the *Wall Street Journal* and insist she discuss the articles with you.

●

You point out that you can't tell who is truly rich just by the cars they drive or the clothes they wear. But that's a good way to tell who's in debt.

●

You explain that poverty comes
when you live above your means.

●

You show your kids that a percentage of
their money should be used to glorify
God so God can continue to bless them.

●

You preach the biblical truth that with
God's blessings come much responsibility.

●

You are continually trying to convince a
thirteen-year-old that you're not rich.

YOU KNOW YOU'RE A DAD WHEN YOU REALIZE YOU'RE RAISING GOD'S CHILDREN

You know you're a dad when . . .

You decide it's time to step up your spiritual game. Because this will impact how your raise your family.

•

Your prayers get serious. Now you pray for your wife and unborn child—ceaselessly.

•

You use your moral authority about TV, computer games, movies, and clothes.

•

You're forced to explain death. Of a pet. Of a grandparent. Of someone even closer.

•

You sometimes go to bed scared.
But grateful God's in charge.

•

You strive to be a man of character. So
you can raise children of character.

•

You teach this truth: if we depend on our
own strength and successes to feel good
about ourselves, we'll be unprepared for
the difficult days all of us inevitably face.

•

You talk to your kids regularly
about their real Father.

•

You talk about war. Why it's horrible.
Why it's been around since Old
Testament times. Why it still happens.

•

You take your kids with you to
feed the hungry at a shelter.

•

You and your kids go on a mission
trip to a Third World country.

•

You teach that when you feel
the worst about yourself, it's
time to serve other people.

•

You insist the family go to worship
services. You give no quarter here.

•

You feel a kind of joy when your kids show kindness to others.

•

You teach your kids to laugh at their mistakes. Not dwell on them.

•

You realize your child's spiritual condition more than anything will determine the path he takes in life.

•

You say prayers at the bassinet. Then at the crib. Then at your child's bed.

•

You teach your child the Ten Commandments. And live by them.

•

You read the Bible to your children and are proud when your twelve-year-old knows exactly where to find Deuteronomy.

•

You allow a child to experience pain. Because that's the only way he'll grow spiritually.

•

You remember the big picture: your children won't remember or care whether they were bottle-fed or breast-fed, whether Mom had an epidural or a drug-free birth, or whether they made their grand entrance at home or in the hospital. They will remember the love in the family and the values their parents taught them.

•

You are the spiritual rock of the family.
This requires a supernatural Resource.

•

You teach that true happiness doesn't
depend on our things but our thoughts.

•

You teach that success isn't a guarantee
or a right. But a consequence. And
sometimes an undeserved blessing.

•

You sometimes have to ask God for
the strength to keep your hands
off your older kids' problems.

•

You influence your kids' ability to form healthy, happy relationships by having a strong and healthy relationship with them.

•

You realize you can't talk to your children about faith and God unless you yourself are living a moral and spiritual life.

•

Your wife or child is hospitalized and you have to learn what "trusting God" really means.

•

You trust God enough with your resources that you tithe back to Him, even if you don't have very much.

•

You believe your faith starts in
the home, not in the church.

•

You convince your kids they're significant.
Because they're God's children.

•

You teach your kids that life is unfair.
And that's one of God's greatest gifts to
humanity. Because we usually receive
so much more than we deserve.

5

YOU KNOW YOU'RE A DAD WHEN YOU THINK DIFFERENTLY THAN MOMS

You know you're a dad when . . .

Your goal is to help even the shiest
kids find their courage.

•

You have more confidence in your kids
than they have in themselves. And you
know your job is to build their confidence.

•

You realize too late that the only way to
avoid sibling rivalry is to avoid siblings.

•

You tell a child she can figure out a
problem herself. Then you spend the next
eighteen years holding your tongue when
you want to jump in and fix things for her.

•

You remind your kids that confidence comes by overcoming.

•

You're no longer interested in being an urban pioneer. Now you want a safer neighborhood for the kids.

•

You admit your screw-ups but don't dwell on them.

•

You try to explain to a panicked mom that glue is edible. Sort of.

•

You understand that food stolen off
your plate tastes better to your kids
than any other food in the world.
Sort of the way you feel about stealing
food off their mother's plate.

•

You wish you knew how to fix stuff.
Because then you could teach your
kids how to fix stuff. So instead, you
teach them who to call to fix stuff.

•

You regale your kids with stories
of adventure and bravery.
Somehow, sometimes you become
the hero of the story.

•

You wonder if the first grade
teacher, who looks twelve, can really
teach your child how to read.

•

You take your kids hiking. Even
if it's just through the nearby
woods or across the street.

•

A game of catch is waiting for you at home.

•

You discover your kids have created a
superhero avatar of you, and you like it.

•

You regularly teach your child
to hold out her right hand and
introduce herself. Careers have been
derailed by failure to know this.

•

You have the ability to make your kids laugh like nobody else can.

•

You dodge the question when they ask you to explain the lyrics of the song they heard you listening to.

•

You let your kids drink Coke at breakfast when Mom isn't looking because it keeps them quiet and they're going to school and the teachers will be able to handle them.

•

You buy sleeping bags and a tent to "camp" outside with your kids in the backyard. Then, at 11:00 p.m., everyone is driven inside by the bugs.

•

You decide to teach them how to do chin-ups. Then you realize that, well, you're not in as great a shape as you thought.

•

You take your kids to a farm and show them how to feed a cow without losing any fingers.

•

You take your kids on a bug hunt in the nearest available woods.

•

You encourage individual creativity by applauding his artistic efforts even if you have no idea what that blob he just painted is supposed to be.

•

You regularly give the Homework Talk.
No TV, no video games, no phone calls,
no laughter, no jokes, no Cokes, only life-
sustaining liquids until homework is done.

•

You watch for your child's hidden gifts
and talents to surface. And as soon as
you spot one, you hire a private tutor.

•

You challenge your kids to hit you
in the stomach. Until one day . . .

•

Over Mom's strident objection, you
take your kids to the go-cart track
because you really want to drive one.

●

You buy your kids a chemistry set.
The first experiment you teach them
is how to make blue fire. The next one
is how to use a fire extinguisher.

●

You take along a book on birds whenever
you take your kids to the park. That way,
instead of saying, "I have no idea what kind
of bird that is," you say, "Let's look it up."

●

You realize the high school years
will be much more enjoyable if good
manners are enforced at age three.

●

You start encouraging your child
to work things out without you.
And then find yourself continually
jumping back in the mix.

•

You realize you have the power to define
their future by what you tell them now.
If you tell them they are smart, they
will believe you. If you tell them they
are stupid, they will believe that too.

•

You take your kids to the woods and
teach them where to cross a stream.
And you tell them that in life, there will
be a great many streams to cross.

•

You teach your second-grader chess. And continue to play him after he starts beating you.

•

You wake up from a dead sleep because you realize college is only ten years away and you haven't saved a dime.

•

You teach them how to ride a bus, take a train, and hail a cab. These are life skills they need to know.

•

Your kids work on the computer in the den, where everybody can see the screen. Even you . . . from the couch.

•

You teach them they'll meet bullies in the lunchroom, in a chat room, on the playground, even in the executive suite. And bullies hate to be stood up to.

•

You teach kids it's foolish to argue about something they can find the answer to on the Internet.

•

You show your children how to cook your grandfather's favorite chili. This lesson is followed closely by a dose of Tums.

•

Your child asks you if you know where you're going, and you reply that you've only been driving thirty minutes.

●

In an attempt to impress your kids
with your skateboarding skills, you
wind up with your leg in a cast.

●

You're sitting in a movie theater with two
dolls on your left, a teddy bear on your right,
and a sleeping seven-year-old on your lap.

●

You laugh at yourself in front of
your kids. They'll learn they can
laugh at their mistakes too.

●

You inform kids there is no clean underwear
fairy. And they can't wear yours or Mom's.

●

You teach your kids not to interrupt.
Especially you. Or their mother. Or
their teachers. Or even their siblings.

•

You teach kids that our soldiers deserve
our love, gratitude, and prayers.

•

You lecture about money and how it's
earned and how a lot of things need
to be done around the house that
you might be willing to pay for.

•

You allow your kids to beat you in a race.

•

Suddenly, you're legitimately outrun by a ten-year-old, and you don't know whether to feel pride or start taking vitamins.

•

You introduce the concept of responsibility—and live it in front of your kids.

•

You take your kids into the voting booth with you.

•

You explain democracy at the dinner table. And how, for instance, the family is a benign dictatorship.

•

You teach that one of the biggest
barometers of future success is the ability
to practice delayed gratification.

•

You recognize when a zombie-eyed child
has been in cyberspace too long and
it's time for her to rejoin the family.

•

You take the kids for a long walk
in the woods and then idly wonder
if you just might be, well, lost.

•

You explain to your seven-year-old
that you forgot what poison ivy looks
like and now you both know, and
please pass the calamine lotion.

•

You test drive a Corvette with
an ecstatic copilot.

•

You build confidence in your kids. And
notice that doing so curiously builds yours.

•

You're strict about family-safe
computer games, but drool over
the newest PlayStation.

•

You stay up late at night practicing
your kids' computer games so you
can beat them the next day.

•

You tell stories about how you had
to mow yards when you were six
to earn money for college.

•

You teach that actions speak louder than
words. Trust isn't given; it's earned.

•

You light up thinking you've spawned
another Louie Armstrong when
some band teacher says your child
has perfect French horn lips.

•

You enforce the rule "Grades come
first," and you're thankful your kids
can't see your old report cards.

•

You confess that while you never learned the piano, it's important they do. And tell them they'll thank you for it in fifteen years.

•

You learn regretfully that your kids don't really care anything about your baseball card collection.

•

You know who their best friends are. And what they're really like.

•

You have your kids take cards off the Angel Tree so they'll learn about giving to others.

•

You actually talk to other dads you
work out with about raising kids
rather than about the business
deals you closed that day.

●

You give the "you're going to have to raise
your game for middle school" speech.

●

You think clothes for young girls have run
off the rails. Your daughter doesn't agree.

●

One day after riding roller coasters
with your kids, you realize that
only idiots or kids would put their
life in jeopardy like that.

●

You have to explain to an excited
fourteen-year-old why the speedometer
goes up to 160 but the legal speed limit
is 70. And he can't drive over 40.

•

Just so you'll look wise, you stay
up at night searching the Internet
for answers to questions your child
asked but you couldn't answer.

•

You show your son how to use a
lawn mower. And plan for the day
when he will do it all by himself.

•

You challenge your kids to a "hold your breath
under water" contest only to realize your
kids would rather drown than let you win.

●

You are the show-and-tell project at school.

●

You come to the conclusion—after you had to drive to soccer, dance, gymnastics, piano, tutoring, art class, and then to karate—that your kids might be overscheduled.

●

You teach your child how to have a conversation with an adult. That means more than a "yeah" or "uh huh." Eye contact is good too.

●

You forgo *Game of Thrones* on TV to sit with your kid while he writes his paper on the Renaissance and Reformation.

●

You encourage friendships with kids
who look and sound different.

●

You listen quietly and let your
child teach you every single thing
she learned in class that day.

●

You watch your twelve-year-old
standing in your bedroom, flexing his
muscles, asking you to look at them,
and you tell him there's really nothing
to look at. Your wife elbows you.

●

You explain to your kids that you don't have to be great at something to enjoy it. Golf is an example. Most people stink at it but love it anyway.

•

You spot glimpses of the awesome adult your child could become.

•

You see athletic potential in a six-month-old.

•

You agree to coach a sport you know nothing about because it's the only way your child will get on a YMCA team.

•

You celebrate his first home run but teach that a successful life is made up of hitting a bunch of singles.

●

You install a hoop in the driveway with the full knowledge that one day your kid will beat you like a drum.

●

You destroy your kids at Wiffle ball and explain to your wife that kids need to learn to deal with competition.

●

You realize that fatherhood is about balls—baseballs, footballs, soccer balls, dodgeballs, basketballs, tennis balls, and other spherical or semispherical objects.

•

You review the intricacies of the
double steal with a six-year-old
who just wants to play catch.

•

You paint your stomach purple and
stand shirtless in January while
you yell for your child's team.

•

You put aside your competitive spirit
because what really matters to a team of
five-year-olds are the cookies and drinks
after the game. They don't care who won.

•

You feel guiltier over missing
your kid's game than missing a
business review meeting.

•

You worry your child will land on a
psychiatrist's couch because you missed
a third-grade volleyball game.

•

You suffer anxiety, night sweats, panic
attacks, and short-term memory
loss during your child's tryouts.

•

You learn your pain is not your child's
pain. If his failure to make the team
bothers you more than it does him, it's
time to reevaluate your priorities.

•

You take your dainty little princess to a hockey game and learn she loves the fights.

•

You teach kids which team to cheer for. They'll buy this when they're young.

•

You take your baseball glove to a major-league game and tell your skeptical wife you want to catch one for the kids.

•

Playing with older kids makes you play harder. Advil is called for later.

•

You jog with your kids and realize
they're showing you mercy.

•

You enforce pregame curfew.

•

You give a seven-year-old
pregame pep talks.

•

You pay for ski lessons to keep your five-
year-old out of your hair—and learn at
the end of the week that he flew down
a double black diamond while you
were inching down the bunny slope.

•

You tumble down a mountain—losing skis, poles, gloves, and glasses—because you stupidly agreed to race your kids.

●

Standing on the sidelines, watching your athlete, you realize it's as far as you can go. This pretty much explains fatherhood.

●

You buy a soccer ball and ask your child to autograph it.

●

You teach them not to argue with the referee or they'll never get the close calls.

●

You spend your anniversary weekend in one state, cheering for your daughter while your wife is in another state, cheering for your son.

●

You can justify the cost of a club team as a way to land a scholarship.

●

You realize, years later, the odds of an athletic scholarship were slim and none.

●

You think a family vacation is a good idea before you load everybody up for a ten-hour car trip. After thirty minutes and two stops, you wonder . . .

●

You take the family on a vacation and tell them to not worry about money, then worry about money the whole trip.

●

You point out the scenery even though no one wants to be interrupted from their video games and texting.

●

You agree to go to Disney World. And once there, think you've entered the seventh circle of hell.

●

You've spent $6,000 on a ski vacation, $10,000 on a trip to Europe, $5,000 on a trip to Disney World—and what your kids remember most fondly is a trip to a state park that cost $212 including tips.

●

You arrange bulkhead seats on airplane trips because you know the mountain of kid stuff you will be bringing onto the plane.

●

You buy an expensive video camera to record the vacation, see no reason to read the directions (because, hey, you're a guy), and somehow erase all the video. But, thankfully, the sound is still there. So it's weird radio.

●

You're excited about an eighty-dollar-a-day kids' ski camp as long as the instructors wear them out.

●

You allow yourself to be buried in sand
from the neck down. And then watch
your kids get distracted and wander off.

●

You decide that for everyone's mental
health, the kids get their own hotel room.

●

You have everyone in the family run their
hands over the Vietnam Memorial.

●

You stand above the USS *Arizona*
in Honolulu so your kids can see
just how much freedom costs.

●

You take your kids fishing in a mountain stream where you insist the fish are biting and, after four hours of serious complaints about catching nothing, try to shift the conversation to the joy of being outdoors.

●

You take the whole family to New York City. You walk the local neighborhoods, take the subway, see the Statue of Liberty, and grab a Yankee game. Then you take your family to Ground Zero. And tell them it's okay to cry.

●

You shell out big bucks for a deep-sea fishing trip, but not four dollars for the over-the-counter seasickness medication you think is too expensive. You regret that decision.

●

In an effort to guarantee fish, you take
your kids to a stocked pond, where you're
given bait and rods. You come home
with happy kids and even some fish.

●

You forget about all the fussing
in the backseat and think this
trip was the best ever.

●

You realize your wife makes
you a better dad.

●

You take time off to be alone with Mom.

●

You remember that kids come and go. Your relationship with your wife shouldn't.

•

You worship the ground their mother walks on.

•

You're affectionate with your wife in front of the kids. They say they hate it. Kiss her again.

6

YOU KNOW YOU'RE A DAD
WHEN YOU REALIZE THAT
FIFTEEN-HOUR DAYS
AT WORK ARE EASIER
THAN FIFTEEN-HOUR
DAYS WITH THE KIDS

You know you're a dad when . . .

You realize the only place you can relax and read the news is at work.

•

You excuse yourself from an out-of-town business dinner so you can call home to say good night to your kids.

•

The picture of your kids on your desk is five years old, but you can't bring yourself to exchange it for a newer one because they were so cute when they were small.

•

You interrupt a meeting to pick your child up at the child care center—and feel glad that Mom couldn't do it.

•

You wonder if your kids are proud of what you do for a living. Do they even know what you do for a living?

•

You show up to eat with your child in the school cafeteria for lunch. And bring McDonald's.

•

You take the afternoon off to take your daughter to a museum.

•

You weigh the impact of a promotion on the time you spend with your family.

•

You come home, eat dinner with your kids, kiss them good night, then go back to work.

•

You realize that putting the family first means sometimes you have to put work first.

•

You quiz HR about family-friendly policies.

•

You don't let your work define you. You're more than an accountant for an international corporation. You're a dad.

•

You teach your kids there's honor in hard work. Whatever it is. That a server deserves as much respect as a CEO.

•

You discuss the ups and downs of your career with your kids as they get older. So they'll remember you overcame struggles to get where you are.

•

After telling people what to do all day— you have a three-year-old tell *you* what to do on the weekend. That's why you're sitting on the floor in a silly Spider-Man cape.

•

You teach them to do what they're good at until they can do what they love.

•

You're there when your kids really need a dad.

•

You don't care who breathed on who, who pinched who, or who made a face at who—you want peace over justice. So you discipline *all* the participants.

YOU KNOW YOU'RE
A DAD WHEN EVEN
THOUGH YOU STAY
AT HOME, YOU'RE NOT
MR. MOM. YOU'RE DAD.

You know you're a dad when . . .

You learn the new lingo of SAHD, WAHD, and WIHF. If you don't know what any of this means, then you're not one of them.

•

You have to answer the question "Where's Mommy?" all day long.

•

You're talking to clients over the phone and aiming the remote control at *Shrek* while your toddler drools on your laptop.

•

You realize days filled with marketing meetings, interoffice politics, and sales quotas are a cakewalk compared to days

filled with diaper changes, shopping
while holding on to a squirming six-
month-old, and temper tantrums.

•

You can throw dirty diapers
on top of your ego.

•

You can't share the good news about
a Swiffer WetJet with just any man.

•

You're asked by a woman at
the grocery store if you dressed
your children by yourself.

•

You realize a good part of the locker room can't identify with you.

•

Soccer moms regard you as a hero.

•

A diaper company sends you a personal e-mail wishing you "Happy Mother's Day."

•

You can truthfully say to yourself, "The most important things to me are my kids."

8

YOU KNOW YOU'RE A
DAD WHEN HIGH SCHOOL
GRADUATION MEANS
BEING TERRIFIED OF THE
NEXT FOUR YEARS

You know you're a dad when...

You finally accept that even though
you've spent thousands and thousands
of dollars on softball leagues, soccer
teams, volleyball coaches, piano tutors,
and violin lessons, they're not going
to get any kind of scholarship.

•

**You tell your kids college isn't for
everybody. But growing up is.**

•

You finally tell your kids all the
wild things you did in high school.
Now that they've graduated.

•

You see that in spite of nursery school, kindergarten, six years of grade school, two years of middle school, and four years of high school, they're totally incapable of filling out a college form without Mom's help.

●

You get excited about the fact that hundreds of thousands of dollars in scholarships go unclaimed every year.

●

You finally realize it's easier to come up with $25,000 a year than it is to qualify for one of those unclaimed scholarships.

●

You start writing budget-busting checks just to apply to college! You're amazed that some colleges charge $100 to apply.

•

You refuse to fund a four-year music appreciation degree.

•

You tell your kids that at the end of the day it doesn't matter what college they go to. Just come home with a degree.

•

You put off funding your 401(k) for as long as you have a child in college. Maybe longer.

•

You google your kid's roommate if you don't know him.

•

You suggest that if everything they packed for college doesn't fit in the car, it won't fit in the dorm.

•

You're being hit up for $3,500 for a campus meal ticket.

•

You tell your college student to guard that meal ticket as if it were a fake ID.

•

It strikes you during campus parent orientation meetings that your son may not be at freshman orientation. He could be working on his tan.

●

You make sure your freshman can find her way around campus. And know that after you leave, she still won't know where she is.

●

You first realize your daughter is moving to a coed dorm when she tells you the person next door is "hot."

●

You bring your tool kit to dorm move-in day.

●

You tell your freshman that the most important building on campus is the career center.

•

You understand their relationships
with the opposite sex will now
get a lot more complicated.

•

You buy yourself a college T-shirt
and wear it around campus in spite
of your kids begging you not to.

•

You drive home in tears after
dropping her off at college.

•

You buy season tickets for your son to
attend his college football games. And learn
later he didn't make it to a single game.

•

You put your college kids on a budget.
And tell them if they need something
besides books and food, "That's
why God created student jobs."

•

You're constantly told that other
parents give their kids more money.

•

You tell them that selling their books for
party money means they'll be living at
home next semester and working full-time.

•

You work twelve hours a day, drive
a ten-year-old car, and take out a

second mortgage just to pay for college—only to have your daughter tell you that school is killing her and she needs a vacation in Cabo.

•

You show up for Parents' Weekend only to learn your kids have left town.

•

You pray your kids won't do the idiotic things you did in college.

•

You reassure them there's honor and glory in struggling for good grades on little money and sleep.

•

You suggest your kids start studying before
10:00 p.m. It's a useless conversation,
but you feel better afterward.

•

You encourage them to get to know their
professors and to talk to them regularly.
Tell them not to wait until finals to do this.

•

You give advice when asked for money.

•

You listen to your daughter talk all about
her classes. Even when she's trying to
explain why organic chemistry is cool.

•

Your daughter calls in tears saying she hates college because she has no friends, and you want to do something, but her mom says she's just broken up with her boyfriend. So you know to do nothing.

●

You tell him you will not pay for him to take acting classes.

●

You encourage her to join all the clubs relevant to her major. This is where contacts for future jobs are made.

●

You're told she can't stand living in a dorm, that the coolest kids live in apartments. But you're not swayed.

•

Your idea of summer is them getting
a job, and their idea is traveling
to Europe. On your dime.

•

You have a political argument with
someone who gets his opinions
from Comedy Central.

•

You tell your son he needs to pay for any
course he drops because he's failing.

•

You remind her that summer internships
lead to jobs after graduation.

•

You dread two words: *spring break.*

•

Your twenty-two-year-old wants you
to dress like you're twenty-two.

•

You're tossing down your stool softener
about the time your daughter finishes
doing her hair to go out for the night.

•

You tell him there will be no big
gift at college graduation because
he just got a $150,000 present.

•

You're happier than your college
student at graduation. He won't
understand your giddiness.

●

Your college graduate tells you she's thought about it, and she doesn't want to move out of your house for at least two years.

●

You say it doesn't matter if he finds a job or not; either way, you're cutting the money off.

●

You encourage your kids to chase their dreams. On their nickel. Or dime.

●

You say graduate school is a very adult idea. And adults pay their way.

●

You listen to your college grad complain that his first paycheck doesn't begin to pay for his lifestyle. And treasure that moment.

●

You remind her to never let time or distance get between them and her friends.

●

You remind your kids to not go into the future without God. It's a very scary place.

9

YOU KNOW YOU'RE A DAD
WHEN YOU REALIZE THAT
NO MATTER HOW OLD
THEY GET, THEY WILL
ALWAYS NEED THEIR DAD

You know you're a dad when . . .

Even though you sometimes wish
they were still little, you raise
your kids to live without you.

•

You learn the fine art of letting go.

•

You tell your kids they can go to
Los Angeles or New York to chase
their dreams—but they pay.

•

**You ask your adult kids how
their prayer life is.**

•

You are amazed at what your children have become. And tell them so.

•

You threaten your kids with the reminder that one day they'll be taking care of you.

•

You call your business friends and ask them to interview your college graduate.

•

You help them set realistic expectations after graduation. Like, don't expect to buy a Lexus if you can't even afford an apartment that doesn't leak and a car that runs.

•

You urge your kids to make
the world a better place.

•

You encourage your kids to read something
more than text messages, like: business
books, the Bible, and great literary classics.

•

You dare your kids to dream big.

•

You recognize that college may
not be for them, so you show them
your electrician's huge house.

•

You encourage them to see the countries
whose names they can barely pronounce.

•

You continually remind them of their gifts.

•

You teach them they can be an instrument of God by helping those less fortunate.

•

You teach them that the most valuable asset they can have as they enter the adult world is their integrity. A good handshake doesn't hurt either.

•

You encourage your kids to live fearlessly.

•

You reassure them that 90 percent of the things they're most scared about will never happen. And God will give them the power to deal with the rest.

•

You encourage your kids to live for a noble cause.

•

Your kids know you will always love them.

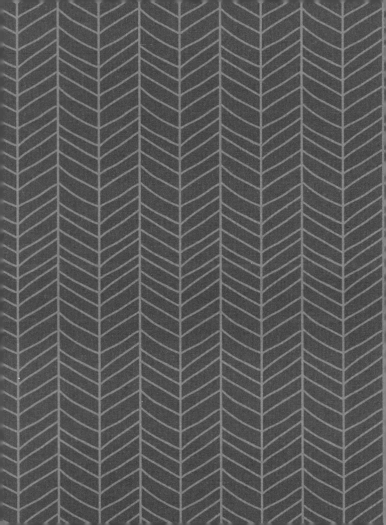